SOCCER

by Tessa Kenan

TABLE OF CONTENTS

Words to Know........................2

Let's Play Soccer!........................3

Let's Review!........................16

Index........................16

tadpole books

WORDS TO KNOW

ball

cleats

field

goal

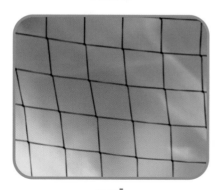
net

team

LET'S PLAY SOCCER!

soccer field

Let's go to the field!

This is my team.

We wear blue.

5

Their team wears red.

We play!

soccer
ball

We kick the ball.

cleat

We wear cleats.

net

We kick the ball into the net.

Goal!

We win!

Good game!

LET'S REVIEW!

Point to the soccer ball. Can you name the other sports equipment shown below?

INDEX

ball 9, 12

cleats 11

field 3

goal 13

kick 9, 12

net 12

play 8

team 4, 7